Recycle Your Gladrags

How to find and repair old clothes

By

Dee Maldon

Bookline & Thinker Ltd.

Bookline & Thinker Ltd
#231, 405 King's Road
London SW10 OBB
www.booklinethinker.com

Recycle Those Gladrags – How to find and repair old clothes

This book is a work of non-fiction
A CIP catalogue record for this book is available from the British Library

ISBN: 9780956517722

Printed and bound by Lightning Source UK
Book cover designed by Donald McColl

Charity shops are full of promise – especially for those who want to wear something unique. But these shops can also be overwhelming. Browsing through their rails of clothing can take time and patience.

Dee Maldon offers an overview of fashion history, along with advice on how to examine clothes, how to remove old stains and odours and how to revamp the clothes you find.

This book is essential for the girl who wants to wear great gladrags without paying vintage or designer prices.

Contents

Introduction

It was in the 1960s and '70s that independent-minded young women moved away from the cookie-cutter styles of the high street to seek unique fashions from the past. I think of myself as being quite mainstream in fashion, but I fondly remember the mink fur coat I picked up at Paddy's Market in Glasgow. I remember feeling very Abba although I don't remember Agnetha ever wearing fur. But the fur coat was a hugely liberating experience because I could wear flimsy clothes in winter. The coat's warmth stretched from my neck to the heels of my boots so I had no fear of Scotland's harsh winter winds. I also remember buying a 1940s black chiffon dress that was eight sizes too big. My figure swam in it, but I loved the fabric and the style. I couldn't simply leave it in the charity shop.

Thankfully, the shop's volunteer suggested I find a tailor and, without further consideration, I took it to a dressmaker who tailored the dress to my figure. I felt like the belle of the ball and called my charity shop dress a 'gladrag' because it made me happy.

The fact is that whatever you find in a charity shop is likely to be unique, no other shop will have it in stock – this year, at least! Another major consideration is that clothing from previous eras was often better quality than that made today. For instance older silks don't wrinkle and the surfaces of older woollens don't erupt with tiny balls. Also women of yesteryear valued their clothes. They had to save hard as a dress cost a huge amount in relation to income. As a result, a fancy frock was truly for a special occasion. At home, women often wore older clothes, keeping 'good' clothing for trips outside the home. In addition, they knew how to care for fabrics. 'Good' clothing never went into the washing machine. That was an absolute no-no.

Also we can't forget that manufacturing isn't as good as it once was. Clothing manufacturers today know we will wear clothes only for a short time before tossing them aside. Previously far more man hours went into each garment; hence the price of clothing was high in relation to income.

Charity shops can be an Aladdin's cave of opportunity for those interested in fashion. But, for the uninitiated, it is hard to know where to start, what to look for and how to shed any stains and smells.

For those who want to give charity shops a try and possibly even alter what you buy, then read on, this books for you!

Dee

Recycle Those Gladrags

Terminology

Retro – refers to clothes that are copies past fashions. These clothes are not in themselves 'old'.

Vintage – definition varies from simply 'past fashion' to anything that is up to 100 years old.

Antique – technically an antique has to be 100 years old. Sales of antique clothing are generally made by collectors and dealers and they are not meant to be worn. The age of these fabrics makes them delicate, so care and storage is of vital importance.

Types of old clothing

Haute Couture – designer quality of the highest kind. This was often hand made from the very best fabrics and has exceptionally detailed styling and tailoring.

Ready to wear – Also known as prêt-a-porter, this is bought from a shop.

Dressmaker – commissioned from a dressmaker and designed to fit a specific person

Where to shop

Vintage shops are amazing places to browse. They are like dress museums except you can buy the clothes on display. Unfortunately, the clothing here is often very expensive. However vintage shops are great places to explore and learn about gladrag clothing.

Vintage clothing websites again are great places to browse and learn about former fashions. You can learn the styles of former eras as your fashion taste is broadened. A halter-neck jumpsuit might seem far-fetched at the beginning, but the more you look at it the greater the appeal.

Flea markets are a thing of the past in many cities. They were the domain of the old rag and bone man who used to ride our streets with a horse and cart, swapping old clothes for balloons and sweets. But now he buys in bulk from charity shops. He often sells his goods to traders in Africa and Eastern Europe. But you may still find a regular stall holder in a weekly market. Some of their clothing comes from house clearances. Many of these dealers know their fashion and often set prices high. So look for flaws in the garment and be prepared to bargain.

Also beware of fake vintage clothing at these market stalls. Casual glance may give it the look of past fashion, but take care to examine the seams and smell that garment.

Vintage clothing shops specialise in old clothes. Some people are turned off because they are over-stuffed with clothing, shoes, bags and jewellery but, for others, this is part of their charm. They offer fun when it comes to shopping for old clothes – not just because of what is on offer and the quirky décor they provide, but they also offer a serious opportunity to try out new shapes and styles.

However vintage clothing shops are expensive – sometimes exorbitantly so! But the clothing here is usually in good condition, clean and carries some panache. Owners of these shops work hard scouring estate sales and auctions to ensure they have stock worth purchasing. Vintage clothing dealers will starve unless their stock is chic and wearable. Many of these traders are not rich, they deal in these clothes because they love them. Visiting their shops will help you gain an appreciation and knowledge of what to look for in charity shops and market stalls.

Vintage clothing fairs bring together small dealers. Shoppers pay an entrance fee but once through the door you will find stalls of clothing and accessories from most eras. Trying things on often involves going behind a screen and sharing space and a mirror with other shoppers. Bartering can be done here because, having transported their clothes, stall holders often don't want to carry them home. Also the stall holders often love their clothes, and they love people who also love their clothes. Shopping here can be very personal and huge fun.

Online shopping offers simple access to a glorious array of clothing and, sometimes, the prices are better than in vintage shops. Online dealers aren't paying rent for a high street shop so their overheads are lower. But as with all online shopping – buyer beware! Ask about refunds if the item doesn't fit or isn't quite as perfect as the website claimed.

The following websites offer a wonderful collection of clothing.

http://www.oxfam.org.uk/vintage

http://www.vintage-a-peel.co.uk/

http://www.myvintage.co.uk/

http://candysays.co.uk/

http://www.marthascloset.co.uk/

Charity shops offer a blend of all of the above. It's worth going to a posh area of town where the donations are likely to be of higher quality. But charity shop organisers are becoming more knowledgeable about fashion, and many charities now instruct volunteers on the type of clothing to charge more for.

A Brief Overview of Fashion

Late 1800s – Victorian era

The middle of the Victorian era saw huge changes to women's clothing, due mainly to two developments. One was the invention of the sewing machine so there was no more need for laborious hand stitching. In addition, dying techniques had improved so that clothing colours could be more dramatic.

It was at this time that the idea of 'designer' or haute couture evolved. Until now wealthy families employed or commissioned gowns to be made by good dressmakers. But in the 1860s Charles Worth, an Englishman, became chief dressmaker to Empress Eugenie, wife of Napoleon III. Her clothes were admired wherever she went. Fashionable women of the time tended toward huge crinoline dresses that were elaborate but cumbersome. Under these were corsets and a series of stiffened petticoats over a steel frame that pushed the dress outward making walking at any speed difficult.

Under advice from Charles Worth, Princess Eugenie gave up these dresses. Firstly he flattened out the front of the gown, and slowly moved the bulk of fabric to the rear to create a vast bustle. His 'Worth' name became synonymous with fashion. Wealthy American women travelled across the Atlantic for his clothes and took home trunks of them. It was the first time a particular dressmaker had such an international impact on the women's fashion.

Women of poorer families, or those who disliked being encased in so much fabric, could wear the Princess Gown. This had a fitted bodice over the breasts, tight collar and sleeves and fell to a loose skirt so that it barely showed a waist. This is typical of the governess style we associate with Jane Eyre films.

Edwardian era to the 1920s

As women sought emancipation and the right to vote, a more tailored suit appeared on the fashion scene. Waists were tiny, especially compared to the shoulders which were exaggerated in size by huge leg-of-mutton sleeves. After the billowing softness of earlier styles, the small waist, huge shoulders and tightly fitted jackets gave women a no-nonsense air.

Many women used embroidery and lace to soften the look.

A huge change for women of the time was the S-curved corset. Until now corsets had pushed the chest and abdomen in and down which restricted breathing and digestion. The new Scurve pushed the chest out while pushing the lower body backward, creating an upstanding S-shaped silhouette. Thankfully the style ended in 1907 and was replaced by a corset that relied less on pushing and thrusting and aimed, only, to make the woman look slimmer.

World War I saw austerity, and women needed clothes they could go to work in. As a result, hemlines were raised, and practical cotton and wool took over from silk. Decorative touches became minimal.

Interestingly, the first bra was patented in 1914. Mary Phelps-Jacobs, an American, created the first design from two silk handkerchiefs connected with baby ribbon as support. The bras were sold as small, medium and large.

1920s

Freedom and glamour were the mark of 1920s clothing. Hair and hemlines became short, flat chests were popular and straight Flapper-style dresses were cheap and easy to produce. Until this time, fashion had been for wealthy women, but now women of lower incomes could indulge in the latest styles. In a quest to look superior, the rich embellished their clothes with fabulous jewels.

The decade began with dress lengths at the calf but, by the mid-1920s, dress hems had crept up to the knees. Asymmetric hemlines became fashionable as waistlines sank lower until they disappeared altogether leaving the shift Flapper dress we think of today.

Bras had slowly become popular, but flat chests were hugely fashionable. As a result, well endowed women bound their breasts with bandages to keep them as flat as possible. Many women simply wore bodices or lacy vests. The aim was to stop the breasts from wobbling while walking or dancing.

The popular shoes of the time were the Mary Jane style with an ankle strap fastened by a button.

Hats were firmly cloche style and clung to the head like a helmet. The hat meant that, for the first time ever, hair had to be short. The tight hat left no room for pins or hair put into a bun (and no respectable woman at this time would have left her hair to hang naturally as it fell). The low brow of the cloche led to women having to tilt their heads upward to see. It also meant they would peer down their nose at any person before them.

1930s

Austerity after the banking crash of 1929 meant fashion lost its hedonistic quality and became more genteel. Hemlines went back to the calf, and skirts were full and feminine. New fabrics such as rayon and nylon offered a cheap alternative to silk. Finely manufactured nylon was developed for stockings which meant they no longer sagged at the ankles.

The cloche hat that hid hair was replaced with flat, plate-like hats that would show curls (new knowledge of chemicals at this time had led to the development of the permanent wave or 'perm').

Clothes cut on the bias, while not new, grew popular, especially when worn by glamorous Hollywood stars. Again dyeing techniques improved so that colours became even more vibrant with turquoise, pinks and violets showing all their hue.

The zip had been developed in 1917, but it had been used only on shoes and tobacco wrappers. Finally, in the 1930s, it became the mainstay of skirts and dresses and out went fiddly buttons, studs and eyelets.

When it came to breasts, it was finally acknowledged that women came in different sizes. Manufacturers began sizing bras by chest and cup size. The overall shape of the bra aimed to lift and separate so that breasts became pointed under clothing.

1940s

War meant that fabrics were rationed and women really had to think about what they wanted or needed. Old clothes were often picked apart to make new ones, and knitted jumpers were unravelled so that the wool could be used for something new.

Clothing in shops was restrained, drab and uniform. It was tough times for clothing designers and manufacturers. Several top designers came together to create the CC41 label (Clothing Control 1941). This resulted in 34 designs of clothing that could be produced with the cloth rations of the time. The clothing was both chic, utilitarian and could be mass produced. Skirts were below the knee and A-line, while jackets were fitted and limited to three buttons.

After the war, clothing rationing continued, and UK fashions were exported to the United States to bring additional income back home. As a result, British women lived with drab old clothes while watching the glamorous women of Hollywood on their cinema screens. They felt the era of make do and mend continued for all but the rich.

1950s

This was the era of sex appeal with pencil slim skirts and tight jackets to show off the full hour-glass figure. In contrast to this risqué look, dresses came with tight waists before flowing out in full swing to emphasise femininity.

Until now teenage girls had dressed like their mothers. But the pencil slim skirts were considered too sexy for teens, so young women were steered toward wholesome full skirts. As a result, the 1950s began the age of the teen. For the first time, a separate fashion was geared toward teenage girls. These skirts were decorated with poodles and worn not with heels, but with flat shoes and ankle socks to give an overall childish look.

The full skirts needed special petticoats to give them the right shape and movement. Some of the best petticoats were boned, others were heavily starched and still others were tiered and worn with a tightly boned bodice to create a slim waist.

No matter whether you chose a pencil slim silhouette or a full-skirted one, every outfit needed gloves for special occasions.

Housework however was done in a wrap dress or pinnie overall. Stockings, or nylons, were expensive, so women either took them off at home or unclipped some of the suspenders while doing housework. This lessened the pull and likelihood of ladders.

But it was all change before the husband came home from work. Magazines of the time advised women to look glamorous for their husbands. Put on lipstick and a nice dress before he is due home for work. Never greet him with a dirty face or smelling of cooking while complaining of the trials of the day, said the *Women's Own*.

1960s

The 1960s saw so much fashion that it needs an entire book. What follows is simply an outline.

The early sixties was actually very similar to the fifties, with full skirts and pencil slim shaping. The only development was that skirts became a little shorter, reaching to just below the knee.

Jackie Kennedy was only 33 when she entered the White House and she had a huge impact on fashion. She originally favoured French fashions but, for political reasons, had to wear American clothes. Thankfully she found an emigrant designer, Oleg Cassini, who Americanised French fashion by keeping colours solid and removing fussy pockets and trim. Jackie's pillbox hats, three-quarter sleeves, stand-up collars and A-shape silhouette became a 1960s standard.

The shift dress became a simple staple of most women's wardrobe in the mid-sixties. The simple A-line shape was flattering to most figures.

By mid-60s the mini was in. No one is sure who started this trend – Mary Quant plus a few French designer all receive credit – but there is no doubt that it took over fashion quickly. But the mini's popularity could not have happened with stockings and suspenders – the look would have been too racy for the time. Instead the mini's popularity came after the development of tights. Legs could be a uniform from the foot up, with no breaks for unsightly suspenders.

Colours and patterns became more daring than ever before with orange, purple, day-glo green all finding favour.

Slim leg trousers had been popular for casual wear. As the decade wore on trouser waistlines sank to the hips, the legs widened to bell-bottoms and the utilitarian working fabric of denim became known as 'jeans'. Loon pants that were tight fitting to the knee, then flaring to the ankle were popular with men and women.

By the late 1960s hippie power was in alongside retro Victorian fashions. Hemlines plummeted to midi (mid-calf) or maxi (full length) giving women options from the mini and taking fashion to all lengths so that almost anything was trendy except clothes from the previous few decades.

Trendy young brides at this time often opted to marry in Victorian-style nightdresses, white and full-length signifying some sense of purity in this hippy age. Laura Ashley did a roaring trade in white nightdresses for brides. Clothes harked back to the past with paisley prints becoming popular as well as tie-dyeing or using batik techniques at home.

1970s

There was no sudden change in fashion when 1970 came around. Instead, the fast evolution of fashion in the 1960s continued for the next few years.

Trousers became more popular but they were teamed with a short dress or waistcoat of the same fabric to create 'the trouser suit'.

Hemlines were up and down with women wearing maxi coats over mini dresses. Often with a large hat that flopped over the eyes. Hot pants were an alternative to the mini. These were worn with or without a bib and braces. Usually they were worn with knee-length boots and tights were always worn, the bare leg look was not considered sexy.

Platform shoes became higher and were unfortunately often teamed with cream tights.

Much of this was inspired by glam rock which was made popular by David Bowie, T Rex and Roxy Music. Glitter, scarves and sequins were designed to catch the eye. Halter dresses became popular for the first time since the 1930s.

Those not following the glam rock look often went for the more peasant styles. This involved ethnic fashion that took in the kaftan, poncho, Afghan coats and cheesecloth blouses – clothes inspired by the trips young people took back-packing around Europe, the Middle East and to India, the early gap travellers.

Those following the peasant style often added their own touch by knitting, crocheting, or patching the garments. Jeans were also made individual with patches and appliqué.

By mid-1970s, fashion became more tempered with tank tops over full sleeve blouses worn with swirly skirts that moved with motion. Big collars were popular for men and women.

Punk came to the forefront in the seventies, an antidote to prescribed and commercial fashion – the philosophy was that no one should make money from designing trends (although many did make money from punk clothing).

Clothes now had attitude that dared onlookers to stare. Torn, shredded and bold – throw away the handbag and carry a kettle instead! Given the nature of punk – conceived and created by individuals in their own home so that no one made a profit – true punk clothing will not be found in any charity or vintage shop.

Recycle Those Gladrags

What to look for

When going into a charity shop or second-hand clothing shop it is easy to be lost in the array of clothing on offer. So take your time, pull each item of clothing out, hold it up and truly examine it.

Silhouette

Sounds simple but the outline of the outfit must work for your shape. The silhouette has long been the identity of fashion. For instance the emphasis in the 1940s was on the waist, while the sixties favoured the legs and the eighties the shoulders. There is no point in choosing gladrags from the 1940s which emphasise the waist if you don't have one. Instead look at your own shape and think about the silhouette that will work best for you. Tall skinny girls look good in anything from the sixties, whereas girls with boobs look good in tailored clothes that cling to the bust. But whether focus is on the shoulders, boobs or hips, the overall shape of the outfit has to work for you. Trying clothes on is almost necessary to assess shape and fit.

Fabric

Fabric design and content has changed massively through the years. Don't be turned off because it doesn't look like anything in the shops right now, think about how it looked in its time and how it might look on you.

If you like the overall shape and colour, then it is time to look closely at the condition.

Examine for signs of wear, tear, stains and smells – yes, that sniff test! If the garment is expensive, ask to take it out to the street to smell. Let's face it, some charity shops do have stale air and taking the garment outside will allow you to test if the outfit has absorbed this.

Tips on removing stains and smells will be provided in another chapter.

Older clothes were made of natural fabrics such as silk, cotton and wool. As mentioned earlier, man-made fabrics such as nylon and rayon were not widely used in clothing until after World War II. While natural fabrics feel wonderful, they can be more difficult to take care of, and any stains can be more difficult to remove.

Look for care instructions as this will tell you how the item should be cleaned and ironed, they are usually stitched into a lower seam. Clothing without care instructions were generally produced before the 1960s.

Lining

Linings provide weight to an outfit and help it hang well.

In the early part of the 20th century all dresses had linings or separate underskirts. However, after the 1960s manufacturers assumed we would buy underskirts or slips to wear with our clothes.

Jackets carried linings until the 1970s. After that, some jackets had half linings but most, especially summer wear, were made lining free.

Ensure linings are not worn or torn. If they are, decide whether they can be repaired or removed. If repair or removal is not possible, can you live with the lining? Does it alter how the clothing sits or feels? Only you can decide this.

Seams

A lack of lining helps you to examine the seams of clothing.

Clothing made prior to the 1960s tend to have wide seams that were parted and ironed flat for a perfect finish. Often times the fabric edges were cut with pinking shears to produce a zigzag edge that would not fray. More upmarket clothing had the seam edges turned over and stitched neatly or they were bound in silk or cotton to prevent fraying. This all created a flat seam that fell neatly into the shape of the garment.

After the 1960s, seam edges were locked together so they could not be easily unpicked. For manufacturers this was less work and reduced the risk of frayed edges.

Seams that are ironed flat can be unpicked and readjusted for size. Seams with sides locked together cannot be unpicked easily.

Labels

Garment labels are like a peak into clothing history as they reflect the style of the time – right down to the written font!

Most labels simply tell the manufacturer, others also mention the department store the item was sold in. Some labels may carry simply a name. This may have been made by a tailor or dressmaker who had a large enough clientele to warrant a label. Clothes without a label were homemade or the product of a freelance dressmaker.

During the 1960s and '70s many boutiques had their own labels, such as Bus Stop, Chelsea Girl and Biba. Although the clothes weren't expensive, they are highly sought after today. Laura Ashley nightdresses were popular as wedding dresses among the 1970s avant-garde.

Designer outfits are always prized high, especially if they are in good condition. But know who the designer is before you buy.

On a more practical level, care labels became compulsory after the 1970s, and manufacturers had to label an item with its fabric content and provide care instructions outlining how to wash, dry and iron the item.

Buttons

Buttons, studs, ribbons and hooks and eyes were the dominant fasteners until the 1930s. Buttons were usually made of natural materials such as glass, bone, tortoiseshell or something equally exotic. Shortages during the war meant that even they were in short supply. As a result, buttons became quite valuable. They were trimmed from outfits and sewn onto others – no one threw buttons away. By the post-war period plastic buttons were developed in all sizes, shapes and colours. Still the trend on changing buttons continued. Be aware when examining clothing that the buttons may not be original.

Zips

Zips began being used in clothing in the 1930s, usually as side seam fasteners. Until the 1960s they were made of heavy metal. After this plastic zips which were lighter became popular. Zips can break, so look for replacement zips in old clothing by examining the thread and stitching holding it in place. If a zip doesn't work it can be replaced.

If the item is an original dress by a well known designer, having a replacement zip devalues the item among dealers. Bear this in mind, and you could get a very wearable bargain.

What size is this?

No one was a size 8 in the 1970s!

There were plenty of thin girls but, quite simply, size 8 didn't exist. If you were small, you bought a size 10 and were happy.

So what has happened? Have women shrunk in size? Hardly!

Instead manufacturers have become sensitive to the fact that we all want to fit into a smaller dress size, and they have simply tagged garments with lower size labels – and we've bought it!

So that size 12 you pick up in the charity shop, may well be a size 10 or even an 8!

Also, don't forget that prior to the 1970s women wore girdles to pull in their stomachs and midriffs. Dresses, skirts and jackets were designed with the girdle in mind. To wear these close-fitting outfits, a modern-day pair of pull-in knickers is almost essential.

Online, many vintage or retro clothing dealers use the measurement of the outfit rather than the dress size. So, know your size. Use an inch-tape (no metric in those days) to record your measurements. Measure the largest circumference of your chest, take a snug record of your waist and, when it comes to the hips, make sure it takes in the fullness of your behind as well as your width.

Stand up straight to take these measurements. It does make a difference.

What condition?

It is rare to find older clothing in perfect condition. Wear, tears, stains and holes are all flaws. Much depends on whether it is repairable or visible, and only you can decide how much work you are willing to put in.

When examining an item in a shop, market or fair, look very closely. Lay the clothing flat and scour it first on the front and then on the back for stains. Hold it up to the light and peer for holes. Look at buttons, zips and ties to ensure they are all present and secure. Peer at the underarms for stains and smells.

Stains

The most common smell is mildew. This comes from nothing other than being stored in a damp area such as an attic or closet on an outer wall. Unfortunately, mildew is almost impossible to remove even on newer fabrics such as polyester and nylon.

Other stains are simply age – something that may not have caused a problem originally but, with time, it has simply 'set' into the fabric.

Before buying an outfit with a stain, look very objectively. Is the stain visible? Will you wear the outfit if the stain doesn't come out? Once you take the item home then it is yours, stain and all.

Treatment of stains

While you may be able to remove the stain, the fabric may be spoiled by water or by the chemical you are using. So before tackling a stain, first do a test on the underside of the fabric, on a hem or a seam, so that any damage will not be visible.

Try blotting the stain out with water:

-   Use tepid water as, depending on the fabric, hot or cold water could set the stain further.

-   Blot with a damp cotton bud. Let it dry and check to see if the water has ruined the fabric. Silks and rayons should not be blotted with water as they will definitely wrinkle and spoil.

If the fabric is hardy, then you may use a little hand-wash detergent (the kind used for cashmere or silks). Again blot with a cotton bud, do not rub.

Old food stains - these may respond to a small amount of dish washing liquid with tepid water. Again, do a test run on a hem or seam.

Ink – try a small amount of rubbing alcohol (check first that it is colourfast by using on an underside of the hem or a seam).

Rust – this may come from a wire coat hanger and shows up as a brownish-red stain. Place kitchen towel underneath the garment and blot with a little lemon juice or white vinegar. Then leave the item outside, preferably in the sunshine. Keep the kitchen towel underneath.

Dark wine stains are almost impossible to remove, but you can try blotting them with a little club soda.

Never forget the power of a good dry cleaner. Ensure the garment can be dry cleaned and have a word with the staff there. They see more stains than anyone, and their judgement can be pretty sound.

Smells

Sometimes the clothing has simply absorbed the smell of the charity shop or flea market. Hang it up outside or in a room with a flow of air.

If an item has been stored in a closed box it may have a musty smell, again airing the outfit can help. If the fabric is hardy, you may be able to put it in the dryer on a 'cool' setting along with one of the 'dry-cleaning sheets' that are supposed to freshen up our clothes. But check the care label first to ensure the fabric is suitable for the dryer.

Mothball aromas need a good dry clean, again check the care label. You cannot go out smelling of mothballs, this is an aroma that has to be eliminated.

Underarm odour may be removed by dapping the underarms with a little mouthwash and letting it air.

Again the dry cleaner can be your very best friend. Have a word, let them take a sniff and follow their advice.

Worn areas

The material on older garments may have become so fragile that it simply tears when handled. There is no hope for this outfit. It will shred like paper when worn.

Sometimes an item might be faded across the shoulders. This is due to wear. It is impossible to correct without having the garment dyed – an expensive and risky route to take. Consider this only if you truly love the design and the material is hardy enough for fabric dye.

If the seams are gaping, this is often due to the fact that the thread has worn out. This problem is easily fixed by stitching the seams back together.

Small holes or wear can be darned over with thread of a matching colour.

Darning is simply a thread weave. First stitch around the hole so that it doesn't become any bigger. Then sew loosely in a left-to-right direction and follow this in a top-to-bottom weave to fill in small holes. You may use a matching thread or, if you are lucky, you may be able to tease some of the fabric's own threads onto your needle and these can be used to weave over the hole.

Another option is to cut a small patch from a seam, hem or inside pocket and sew to the underside of the hole.

Moths

Moths are a huge problem when buying wools and cashmeres. Sometimes there aren't complete holes but grazed areas that look flatter than the raised fabric nap. Use a fine needle and gently draw the small fibres up. Don't pull, simply guide them.

Full moth holes can be a nightmare to darn and, unless you truly love the garment, leave it in the shop.

All moth eaten garments need to be thoroughly cleaned as moth eggs will hatch and eat your other clothes – so be careful not to infest your wardrobe. Send the garment to the dry cleaner or seal it in a plastic bag and place in the freezer for a week.

Zips

A sticky zip can be repaired by running slightly damp mild soap over the teeth. This will lubricate the zip and let it slide smoothly. If the sliding part of the zip still won't move then place a small amount of soap in the direction you want the zip to move, leave it for a few minutes and try again.

If a zip has broken or missing teeth then the zip itself has to be replaced. If you can't do this, there are many high street tailors who can.

Other issues

Knitted items sometimes have loose threads. These can be pulled through to the underside with a fine needle or use a small hook and poke the threads through.

Velvet may have a shiny worn area that looks flat and crushed. Give the wrong side of the fabric a brief steam over a kettle. Follow this with a gentle brush on the velvet side and the fabric may become revived. If this doesn't work you will have to accept the wear and decide if the piece is worth keeping and wearing.

Recycle Those Gladrags

Fur coats

Vintage fur coats can be a gorgeous luxury, but their purchase can be risky.

Smells

It is not unusual for the coat to smell like its storage container, so expect mildew, mould or even cat pee. Ask to take the coat outside the shop so you can smell it in the fresh air. When you get it home hang the coat outside for as long as possible. This should help. A good dry cleaner can also help remove old smells but this can be costly.

Beautiful intact linings mean that it is difficult to know the state of the skin underneath the fur. Give a handful of fur a gentle tug and look at how much hair is left in your hand. A few hairs are normal, but if your hand is left hairy then the skin has dried out. Leave the coat in the shop.

The skin under the lining should be soft and move well. Roll the fabric in your hands and feel the skin under the lining. If it feels dry and stiff, leave it. A good fur should move in soft rolls.

If you find a good vintage fur treat it well. Comb and wipe with a damp cloth in the direction of the fur. Never store in extreme heat or cold. When wet, let it dry naturally.

Taking care of your gladrags

If you want the garment to be more than a one-night outfit, then you are going to have to take care of it. As mentioned earlier, older clothing is more fragile. To take care of an outfit, you have to know what it is made of. Clothing made prior to the 1970s often has no label identifying the fabric, and you need to know whether you are handling silk, rayon or polyester. While polyester can be washed in the machine, silk and rayon should not even touch water or they will be ruined. The problem is even more severe if the garment has beading, sequins or handstitching.

The dry cleaner can be your very best friend by identifying the fabric and cleaning it.

If money is short then you are on your own and, for fabric identification, you will have to do a flame test.

Flame test

Take a few fibres from an inside seam and hold with tweezers over a flame. Use a candle or have a friend hold a lighter or match. Ensure you keep the fabric above the flame, not in it.

Watch how the fabric burns and smell the aroma.

Fabric	Aroma	Residue left
Silk	Burnt hair	Black, round and brittle
Wool	Burnt hair	Bubble like
Nylon	Plastic	Grey beaded, hard
Polyester	Sweet	Black bead
Rayon	Wood	Disintegrates
Cotton	Burnt paper	Grey ash
Linen	Burnt paper	Grey ash

Once you determine the fabric, you will know how to care for it.

Natural fabrics such as wool, silk, cotton, linen

Wool will not crease and can return to its original size when stretched. This means it is a great fabric for tailoring. It is a hardy fabric and wears slowly.

Some wools are scratchy giving people the idea that they might be allergic to it, but it is simply the rough finish of that particular wool. Some wools are beautifully soft. Mohair comes from angora goats, while angora wool originates from a particular breed of rabbit. Camel hair comes from that creature's undercoat and is extremely warm. Kashmiri goats are responsible for cashmere. The softest hair has to be separated from the more coarse hair, hence time and expense which create high costs. Cashmere is often blended with silk or other wools.

There are many basic types of woollen fabrics. The most common type is thick, soft and fuzzy, with little shine. We all know this from scarves, blankets and jumpers.

Worsted wool is smoother and used for smart tailored clothes. It holds a crease, does not sag and does not easily become worn.

Merino wool feels like cashmere and is softer than regular wool.

Tweed is rough, sturdy and often a two-tone colour.

Herringbone is woven in a two tone colour with a distinct sawtooth shape.

Houndstooth check is recognised by its four-point star shapes.

Jersey has a tight knit of fine wool which hangs well and is suitable for skirts, trousers and jackets.

Petersham is thick and waterproof, usually comes in dark blue and was often used in men's outdoor clothing.

Flannel wool is lightweight and often used in children's clothing.

Gabardine is tightly woven, slightly shiny and used in clothes with distinct tailoring.

Cotton is cool and breathable. It can take high temperatures; bleach helps to return it to a brilliant white colour and it can be dyed with relative ease.

Cotton is often treated to give it a different feel.

Oxford is used for shirts, usually with small stripes.

Poplin is a strong weave that is long lasting.

Sateen has a sheen to it.

Flannel has a soft, raised nap.

Seersucker is crinkled in lengthwise stripes.

Gingham has clean checks.

Terry cloth has a loopy pile that makes it very absorbent.

Velveteen has a deep pile similar to velvet.

Muslin is coarse plain cotton, usually in a natural beige colour.

Cotton blended fabrics may not take dye or bleach as well as plain cotton. Be warned and try the dye or bleach on a hem or seam first.

Silk is elegant but immensely strong. It comes from the silkworm. This creature works hard at creating a strong cocoon. Silk can be hand washed and will only shrink if it wasn't washed before the garment was made.

Brocade is embossed, usually with a paisley-like weave.

Chiffon is very light, almost transparent silk. It may include cotton.

Organza is lightly heavier than chiffon.

Georgette is sheer like chiffon but has a crinkly look.

Silk linen has a bubbled look.

Linen comes from the stalk of flax. It is immensely strong and smooth. It is highly absorbent which makes it perfect for hot weather. However it does crease easily and constant shaping into folds will create wear and tear. Like cotton, it can be boiled and takes dyes easily.

Damask is a reversible weave.

Butcher's Linen is heavy and sturdy, traditionally used by French butchers and in the linings of heavy clothing.

Care of your garment

Handwashing

Use specialist liquid prescribed for handwashing 'delicate' fabrics.

Use warm – neither hot nor cold – water.

Do not scrub, wring or twist.

Let it soak for 30 to 60 minutes.

Rinse gently in warm water without wringing or twisting.

Place on a flat towel and roll it loosely to wring out excess water.

Let dry by leaving flat or on a hanger.

While polyesters and newer fabrics can go in the washing machine, NEVER USE THE DRYER!

Personally, I would stick to dry cleaning. After all, you've found a unique item that you want to wear again, it simply makes common sense to preserve it.

Other ways to preserve your garment:

Do not use a hot iron directly onto the garment. Instead use a press cloth and iron the underside.

Use odour-free, clear deodorant and wait 20 minutes between applying it and putting on your outfit. Deodorants can cling to fabric and make it deteriorate over time.

Clean stains off immediately. Leaving a stain will cause it to 'set'.

Brush clothes after wear, especially velvets, wools and anything with a pile. Use a soft clothes brush to remove hair, crumbs etc.

Don't use wire hangers, they can leave your clothes with rust stains.

For skirts or strapless dresses that need grip hangers, place tissue between the fabric and the hanger so there are no marks left on the fabric.

Beaded or sequined clothing should not be hung on a hanger as the weight will pull it out of shape. Instead, fold it in acid-free tissue and store in a drawer or box.

Never put any item of clothing away that is still damp as it will become mildewed if left over time.

When ironing, press on the inside of the outfit if possible. Otherwise, place a cloth between the fabric and the iron. This will protect the fabric from burning and reduce any sheen that comes from the heat.

Moths are tenacious, keeping them away from wool and silk is a continuous task.

Vacuum closets and drawers every six months.

Don't use mothballs, the smell is difficult to eliminate.

Instead use lavender sachets in drawers, and place cedar blocks on closet hangers.

After buying any second-hand wool or silk, dry clean the item or clean it at home and place in a sealed plastic bag in the freezer for a week. This should be done before the item reaches your wardrobe. You do not want to bring moths into your closets.

Accessories

If you don't want to waltz into the evening in ancient gladrags then charity shop accessories are a great way to gain an individual look that says, 'I am unique'.

Hats

For people who love hats, and there are many of us, older hats offer not just style but substance. So much work went into making them that they offer panache never seen in modern day hat wear.

Cloche hats from the 1920s are often too delicate to wear today. The fact that they sat tight and close to the head meant that the material came into direct contact with hair grease. As a result the fabric is more likely to be worn and damaged. But the flatter, plate-like hats from the 1930s and 1950s can often be found in charity shops. They come in all colours and are often decorated with netting, fake flowers or simple beads.

They are held on by elastic that rests at the back of the head below the hairline.

Fedoras can be wonderfully striking, especially when worn with a trouser suit.

Condition

Check carefully the condition of the hat, especially for faded or discoloured segments. These cannot be repaired.

If there is grease and dirt at the hairline, then this may be difficult to remove. If you really want the hat, and it is cheap enough to take a chance on, you can try to clean the grease with some handwash for delicate clothing, a cup of lukewarm water and a soft toothbrush. Rub gently on to the grease and stand to dry.

A brim that is bent may be soothed into place with your fingers.

Steaming can help revive tired flowers or netting. Give the hat a good brush, and then simply hold the hat about 50cms from the spout of a boiling kettle. Let the steam flow into the underside of the hat first, then the brim and then turn the hat slowly so the exterior of the hat is exposed.

Feathers, ribbons, lace or other haberdashery on hats can be replaced to give the item a truly fresh look.

If you are interested in buying a hat on a vintage retail website, then you are going to have to know your head size. Use the mid-point on your brow as the starting point and measure around your head.

Handbags

Handbags are immensely popular among vintage shoppers. No one is sure why. I put it down to women having an ancient gene from our time as prehistoric gatherers when we needed something strong to carry home all the berries we'd found.

Some handbag styles have endured. Think of Chanel's quilted bag with the chain strap, it has been copied so many times through the decades and has never lost its popularity.

Handbags in the Victorian era were small fabric purses, sometimes beaded or embroidered, that hung from the wrist. They were handmade and didn't have to hold very much – husband's held the money that controlled the purse strings.

The 1930s saw the clutch handbag become popular. Its firm structure matched the tailored clothing of the time. Women carried a lipstick, powder compact, mirror and a small purse.

In the 1940s the clutch bag became even larger with a greater range of colours, clasps and linings.

Until the 1960s, handbags were very well made. Women expected to pay a lot in relation to income – only the rich bought on a whim or had more than one handbag per year.

It's usually the lining of an old handbag that shows wear and tear. Check it carefully. Pen and lipstick marks are common and difficult to remove. Therefore you must decide whether you can live with them.

Check the handles of the bag – are they loose or frayed? Ensure the clasp closes properly. You don't want a bag falling open and spilling its contents or falling open and a thief stealing your purse.

A leather bag can be cleaned and polished with saddle soap and shoe polish. Unfortunately cracks in the leather cannot be repaired and are likely to get worse with wear.

Shoes

These are difficult items because, unless bought unworn, they suffer badly in the condition stakes. Toes are often scuffed, heels worn and interiors tatty. And this is without even discussing size.

But if you do find a pair of shoes made prior to the sixties, and they fit, you are likely to find them very comfortable. Heels were placed to give support while walking. Today, heels are often placed where they look trendy, either too far behind the heel or too far forward.

Width was once an important element in shoe size – A was narrow, D was wide. Women, especially those who didn't work or do housework, tended to have narrow feet. Apparently, the pounding of pavements as we walk spreads the width of our feet. I was told this in the United States when I asked why my small British frame always needed wide-fitting shoes. American women drive everywhere. As a result, their feet don't spread the way European feet do.

Regarding condition, leather that is visibly cracked cannot be repaired. Leave these shoes in the shop. To check the stability of the heels, push down on them. If they feel wobbly they will not give the support needed and may even crumble beneath you at an importune moment.

Don't worry about worn heel spikes, they can be reheeled by a good high street cobbler.

When it comes to the shoe interior, frays and flaps can be glued with rubber cement or fabric glue. If the interior is worn and uncomfortable, try adding new insoles.

Dull leather can be cleaned with saddle soap and shoe polish.

Scarves

A great luxury and so versatile – scarves can be used for necks, heads, waists and handbags. Experiment in your bedroom by wearing them as triangular tops – tying the wide part behind you and tucking the V into the front of your jeans. Or even keep as a square, tie one side around your neck and pin the bottom around your waist so it is a backless top.

There are so many shapes, sizes and colours to play with.

Silk scarves feel wonderful against the skin, and older scarves can come in great colours. Check the finish – the best are edged in overturned stitching to help them hang well.

Wash silk scarves carefully in special silk hand-wash detergent, but do a colour test first to ensure the colours don't run.

If you plan to store your silk scarves rather than wear them, wrap them in acid free paper or the colours may bleed.

Jewellery

This is a truly fun part of gladrag shopping. Wearing gladrag jewellery inevitably draws comment and compliments.

Designs are so vast, that we won't even go into trends. Suffice to say, find what you like and examine the quality.

Dust can be cleaned away, but do this carefully or you may cause scratches to metal and stones. It is best to brush the piece with a very soft toothbrush or smooth cloth.

For caked on dirt, do not soak or submerge jewellery. Instead, use a cotton bud dipped in dishwashing liquid. Dab the area gently, leave it to work a few minutes and then wipe with a smooth, damp cloth.

Any greenish spots or discolouration of metals could be verdigris, otherwise known as copper erosion. If it is mild it can be cleaned off with a cotton bud dipped in vinegar. If it is severe the metal is likely to break, so examine closely before making any purchase.

Rust can also show up on jewellery. Rub at rust with baking powder on a soft cloth. Wipe away with a soft toothbrush (keep it dry, you don't want to encourage more rust).

Fake jewels or rhinestones may look dull. This is because moisture has seeped in between the stone and the metallic coating at the back and caused rust. As a result, the shine is gone permanently. In the United States this is known as a dead rhinestone. The only option is to have the stone replaced.

Jewellery clasps should be examined carefully for verdigris, rust, being loose or being too stiff.

A stiff clasp can be helped with a tiny drop of WD-40, leave it for a few moments to creep through the joint and this may help loosen it.

Rusted or clasps coated in verdigris will likely need replaced.

You may need to visit a jeweller to correct bent metals or to tighten a loose clasp.

Necklaces with loose or broken strands can be repaired. If it is a simple and relatively cheap necklace then you can restring them yourself, but buy proper jewellery string as anything else is likely to stretch and gape. Craft shops sell jewellery string.

More expensive necklaces will have knots between each bead. You should take this type of necklace to a jeweller and have it restrung.

Lastly, store your jewellery carefully. Don't simply throw it in a box where pieces scratch, wear and become tangled with each other.

After wearing jewellery, wipe away make-up and wrap each piece in a smooth cloth.

Perfume can be corrosive to jewellery. When preparing to go out, spray your perfume and wait at least ten minutes before putting on your jewellery.

Revamping your gladrags

You might find something that looks interesting but it needs work. Sometimes it is obvious – wear and tear needs to be concealed or threads might be pulled giving the garment a sad look. Examine each piece carefully and decide what can be done.

Holes can be concealed with pearls, bead, sequins or bows. It may look a bit odd if you simply cover the existing holes with a bead or bow, so place many of them in a pattern or randomly around garment to give it a cared for and styled look.

For instance a cardigan or jumper can look very expensive by sewing fake pearls or contrasting sequins across its bodice and sleeves.

Similar tricks can be done to a dress with a ragged hem. A strip of braid around the bottom can provide an even trim and give weight to a dress making it sit better.

If a hole is strategic, over the bust or sleeve, sew a piece of lace over it and on the opposite side so that it looks like fine detailing.

If you want the outfit to look a little punkish, you can exaggerate the tear further or even stitch it with contrasting thread.

Stains can also be covered with braid, ribbon, buttons or bows. I once trimmed a skirt with vertical lines of braid to cover one small stain. It was a lot of work but the cotton skirt was A-line and received such a jolt of life its own designer would never have recognised it.

Reconstructing your gladrags

Sometimes the garment might be in great condition, but it just needs a little something.

A jacket might look better with braid or ribbon sewn around its edge.

New buttons might brighten and modernise an old coat or dress.

Sometimes it is more radical.

I once found a beautiful silk slip. It fit perfectly and I loved how it felt on my skin, but what to do with it? I really wanted to wear it as a dress, but it was fairly see-through. So I bought a cheap underskirt from a shop to wear underneath. I added some dark lace to the bottom and to the bodice of the slip, and it was transformed into a rather chic dress – although it did cause my grandmother to sniff with disdain. All she could see was the old slip, and no amount of lace could transform it in her eyes.

Another tip is to blanket stitch around the edge of a jacket or coat. Blanket stitch is exactly what it says – look at any old blanket and you will see that it is surprisingly easy to do. Simply use thick thread of a contrasting colour and a broad needle. Start on the underside of the fabric and stitch forward, placing your needle away from the edge and drawing it out on the edge to ensure that the thread is caught around the outgoing stitch. It sounds complicated, but I taught myself to do this stitch by simply taking a good look at an existing blanket.

Shirts can be cut to create waistcoats. It helps to have a dressmaker's dummy when you do this. But you can also use a trusting friend to wear the shirt while you carefully cut off the sleeves and then trim the length and button area to create the size and shape you want. You will have to overturn the areas cut to tidy the outfit up and prevent fraying.

Visit your local haberdashery

Haberdashery is an old fashioned term for a shop that sells buttons, ribbons, bows and threads. These shops are a stimulating delight of beautiful trimmings. For instance delicately laced appliqué patches can be sewn on more elegant clothes (I've even concealed burnt iron marks with these patches).

Don't have decoration only on the front of the outfit, it looks weird and lazy. You want to shine from behind!

Find new flowers or ribbons to replace those on old hats.

Add beads, sequins or bows to give shoes or clothing that individual look.

A single rhinestone jewel can revamp a dress.

Add patches randomly to a tweed tailored jacket. This will give a more modern and 'designer' look to what is a well-shaped clothing item.

Embroidery either with direct stitching or embroidered patches, will create a new look.

Sewing on patches, appliqué and sequins is one way of attachment. Another is to use fabric glue. For smaller jobs you can buy fabric glue in a tube. Lay your outfit out flat, with cardboard between the front and back (you do not want the glue to seep through and make front and back stick together). Gently squeeze a glue line to follow where you want the patch or sequins to go. When placing sequins, make them overlap. It looks richer than having the sparingly placed. Sequins can also be bought on ribbons, and this may be easier to sew on.

For a lot of appliqué or attachments, you may want to invest in a glue gun. Read the instructions carefully! Practise using it on paper first. Ensure no children are around (it will draw them).

Rest the glue gun on an old plate when not needed and never ever try to glue something you are wearing – trust me!

Always remember that the outfit is there for you to recreate. Have fun, find your style and wear it with flare.

Other non-fiction titles by Bookline & Thinker Ltd.

Quick, Boil Some Water – The Story of Childbirth in our Grandmothers' Day by Yvonne Barlow

Today we hear stories of over-worked midwives and short-staffed hospitals, but childbirth has never been easy. Our grandmothers gave birth when there were no washing machines, few hot water boilers and heating came from coal carried in from the back yard.

Not Just Bonnets and Bustles – Victorian Women Travellers in Africa by Annie Hore, Eliza Bradley and Helen Caddick

Victorian women were not docile – they were fearless. Eliza Bradley was shipwrecked and captured as a slave until ransomed. Annie Hore crossed Africa with a baby only 11 years after Stanley took the same route. Helen Caddick explored while accompanied only by 25 bearers and a translator who spoke only Biblical English. Read their stories in their own words and learn what adventure used to be.

8 Day Trips From London – A simple guide for visitors who want to see more than the capital by Dee Maldon

A guide for overseas visitors who want to use public transport to explore Stonehenge, Oxford, Cambridge, Bath, Brighton, Windsor, Winchester and Canterbury.

Lightning Source UK Ltd.
Milton Keynes UK
UKOW021257011211

183026UK00002B/1/P